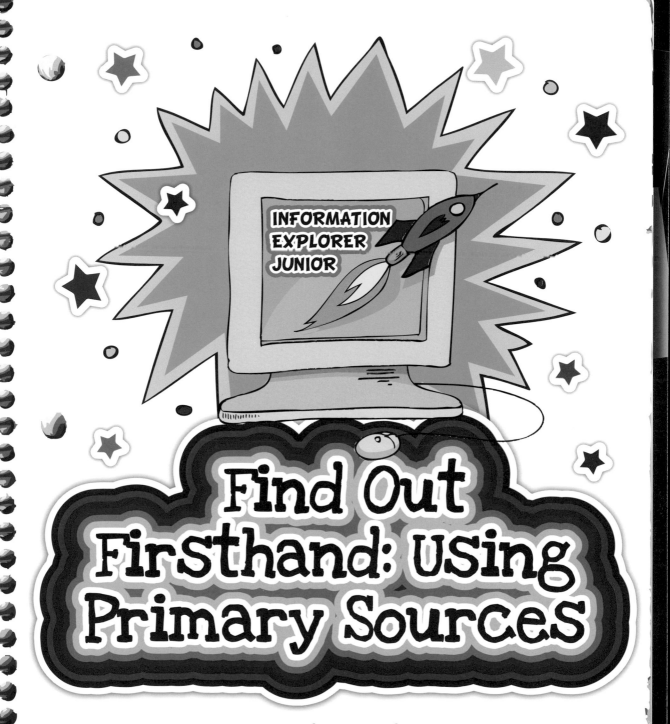

INFORMATION
EXPLORER
JUNIOR

Find Out Firsthand: Using Primary Sources

by Kristin Fontichiaro

CHERRY LAKE PUBLISHING · ANN ARBOR, MICHIGAN

A NOTE TO PARENTS AND TEACHERS: Please remind your children how to stay safe online before they do the activities in this book.

A NOTE TO KIDS: Always remember your safety comes first!

Published in the United States of America
by Cherry Lake Publishing
Ann Arbor, Michigan
www.cherrylakepublishing.com

Content Adviser: Gail Dickinson, PhD, Associate Professor, Old Dominion University, Norfolk, Virginia

Book design and illustration: The Design Lab

Photo credits: Cover, ©Rmarmion/Dreamstime.com; page 5, ©arindambanerjee/ Shutterstock, Inc.; pages 7 and 8, ©Brendan Howard/Shutterstock, Inc.; page 9, ©iStockphoto.com/AVAVA; page 11, Library of Congress, Prints & Photographs Division, National Child Labor Committee Collection, LC-DIG-nclc-00054; page 12, ©Susan Leggett/ Dreamstime.com; page 13, ©Kentannenbaum/Dreamstime.com; page 15, ©Dragan Nikolic/ Dreamstime.com; page 16, U.S. National Park Service; page 17, ©Wimstime/Dreamstime. com; page 18, ©Andrea Haase/Dreamstime.com; page 19, ©Mike Taylor/Dreamstime.com; page 20, ©iStockphoto.com/kali9

Library of Congress Cataloging-in-Publication Data
Fontichiaro, Kristin.
  Find out firsthand : using primary sources / by Kristin Fontichiaro.
    pages cm. — (Information explorer junior)
  Includes bibliographical references and index.
  ISBN 978-1-61080-487-5 (lib. bdg.) — ISBN 978-1-61080-661-9 (pbk.) —
  ISBN 978-1-61080-574-2 (e-book)
 1. Information resources—Juvenile literature. 2. Research--Juvenile literature.
 3. History—Sources—Juvenile literature. 4. History—Research—Juvenile literature. I. Title.
  ZA3070.F656 2010
  001.4—dc23   2012001762

Cherry Lake Publishing would like to acknowledge
the work of The Partnership for 21st Century Skills.
Please visit *www.21stcenturyskills.org* for more information.

Printed in the United States of America
Corporate Graphics Inc.
July 2012
CLFA11

Table of Contents

CHAPTER ONE

Learning from Primary Sources

Have you ever helped friends clean out their garage? What did you find? Old newspapers? Holiday decorations? Old CDs? What about when you clean your room? You might come across old report cards

You never know what you'll find when you clean your house!

Old Town News

Important primary sources are often placed in museums so everyone can visit them.

and pictures. You may also find old clothes that no longer fit you. All those things are **primary sources**.

Primary sources are items that were made during a certain time in history. They include pictures, papers, or objects. These items give us **eyewitness** information about what life was like in the past. You can learn a lot by looking closely at primary sources.

To get a copy of this activity, visit
www.cherrylakepublishing.com/activities.

Activity

Quick! The local TV news wants to do a story about you. Think of three primary sources the reporters could use to describe who you are. Write them down on a piece of paper. What would those things tell people about you? Describe two things that people could learn about you from each item on your list.

CHAPTER TWO

A Picture Is Worth a Thousand Words

Babe Ruth is one of baseball's most legendary players.

A primary source **image** is a picture created during the time or event you are studying. It might be a photo, drawing, or other image. Let's say you are studying the famous baseball player Babe Ruth. You could read about him. But seeing his picture would really make him come to life! You can find primary source images in museums, historical libraries, books, computer databases, and Web sites. Ask a librarian for help if you have any trouble finding images!

Sometimes, images give us answers about life in the past. Other times, we think of new questions. If you are able to, print or photocopy your image. Then you can write notes or questions in the **margins**.

Where is the game being played?

Why is he looking up?

Why are his pants so loose?

Is this a famous moment?

Your family members might have interesting old photos you can analyze.

When we **analyze** an image, it means that we look at the image closely. Try asking yourself three questions about the image.

1. **What do you SEE?** Pretend you are describing the image to someone whose eyes are closed. You should only include facts that you are certain are true in your description. If a man, a woman, and two children are in a photograph, say

"Man, woman, two children." Do not say "Family." They could be two teachers and two students! Later, you might use clues to decide if they are a family. This is called **inferring**.

2. **What do you THINK?** This is when you can infer things using clues in the image. What do you think is happening in the image? Is someone showing off? Being serious? Swinging his bat?

3. **What do you WONDER?** What new questions do you have?

Look at the photo on the next page. This is a photo from the U.S. National Archives. What do you see, think, and wonder? "See" items are red. "Think" items are blue. "Wonder" items are green.

Girl with a suntan

I bet she is outside all day.

What season is it?

Other people far away

Why is she alone?

Is she lonely?

Are there other kids?

Sand

Where is she going?

How long has she been walking?

Bare feet

I think she needs money.

Why doesn't she wear shoes?

Two big boxes

The boxes seem heavy.

How much would they weigh?

What is in them?

Old photos can tell us a lot about the past.

Photographer Lewis Hine took the photo on the previous page. He believed that kids shouldn't work. His notes on this photo say that the girl's name was Rose. She was 10 years old but wasn't going to school. She had been working since she was 7! She carried heavy boxes and babysat for money. This photo is just one of thousands of photos Hine took of child workers. Other people became angry when they saw Hine's pictures. They changed the laws so that kids could go to school instead of work. This all happened thanks to Hine and his primary source photographs!

To get a copy of this activity, visit www.cherrylakepublishing.com/activities.

Activity

It is important to look closely at the facts before inferring. Ask an adult if you can borrow a picture from when he or she was a kid. Now sit down with two or three friends. Do not show them the picture. Describe what you see in the photo to them. Only mention facts! Have your friends write down what you describe.

After you've finished, ask your friends what they think is going on in the photo. Do you agree with them? Do they agree with each other? Why do you think that is? Discuss what facts each of you based your ideas on.

CHAPTER THREE

If These Things Could Talk

Artifacts are another kind of primary source. An artifact is any object that was made or changed by a person. This could be a fancy old vase, your great-grandfather's cooking pot, or your aunt's army uniform.

Almost anything can be an artifact.

This vase belonged to grandma.

It looks very old.

What is the vase made of?

To study artifacts, ask the same three questions:

1. **What do you SEE?** What color is it? What is it made of? What shape and size is it? Is it new? Shiny? Worn?

2. **What do you THINK?** Guess the object's name. What was the object used for?

3. **What do you WONDER?** What questions do you have about this object?

Scientists use special tools to study artifacts.

Look at this photo from the Grand Canyon National Park Museum. At the museum, special **microscopes** help people closely see, think, and wonder about an artifact. The scientist here is taking a close look at a piece of pottery found in the canyon. The pottery has clues about the people who lived there hundreds of years ago, when the artifact was made.

16

To get a copy of this activity, visit www.cherrylakepublishing.com/activities.

Activity

Do you love video games? Video games and game systems are artifacts. Your parents or other adults might have liked video games when they were kids, too. Ask about their old game systems. Maybe they still have one. Or they might have friends who do. They could also show you an online photo. Study the system carefully.

Write down five guesses about how the game system worked. How does a player control the game? How does a player switch from one game to another? Ask the adult helping you if your guesses are correct.

CHAPTER FOUR

Words Can Teach

A **document** is anything that has words. Newspaper articles, letters, e-mails, instant messages, paper money, advertisements, and postcards are all examples of documents. When you use documents as primary sources, make sure that they were created during the time period you are studying. They could be eyewitness accounts of a time or event that were written down later. Look at the documents and ask yourself what you see, think, and wonder.

1. **What do you SEE?** What do the words say? Which words are bigger? Are there images with the text? What do they look like?

2. **What do you THINK?** Who is the author or creator? Which words are most important? What is the message, or the document's main idea? When was the document made? Why was the document made?

3. **What do you WONDER?** What questions do you have about the document?

Activity

Look at a dollar bill. What words do you see in big letters? In tiny type? Whose **portrait** and names do you see? What do the words and picture on the back mean? Write down five questions you wonder about the dollar bill. Ask a teacher, librarian, or other adult to help you find the answers. Are you surprised by what you find? Do you have any new questions?

To get a copy of this activity, visit www.cherrylakepublishing.com/activities.

CHAPTER FIVE

Putting It All Together

The more sources you use, the better your projects will be.

When we **research**, we look at many sources. We use primary sources, encyclopedias, Web sites, books, and more. After you finish your research, you should think about how your

To get a copy of this activity, visit www.cherrylakepublishing.com/activities.

Activity

Sit with a friend and both of your backpacks. Take five things out of your backpack. Ask your friend, "What do you see, think, and wonder about me because of the stuff I carry around?" Now trade places. What can you learn about your friend from the items in his or her pack?

pieces of information fit together. It's a little like a puzzle. What have you learned? If different sources gave you information that wasn't the same or if you still have questions, do more research. That's what the pros do!

Great job, primary source detectives! You're now ready to use primary sources to answer questions and discover new ones. Have fun!

Glossary

analyze (AN-uh-lize) to study or look at something closely

artifacts (ART-uh-fakts) objects made or changed by people

document (DOK-yoo-muhnt) text on paper or saved electronically that gives information or proof of something

eyewitness (eye-WIT-nis) having to do with a person or object that was present at a certain time

image (IM-uhj) a picture, photo, drawing, or painting

inferring (in-FUR-ing) drawing a conclusion after studying the facts

margins (MAR-jinz) blank spaces that surround a text or image on a page

microscopes (MYE-kruh-scopes) instruments that make small objects appear larger

portrait (POR-trit) an image, such as a drawing, painting, or photograph, of a person

primary sources (PRY-mayr-ee SOR-siz) original documents, objects, and other items that were created at the time being studied and that come directly from witnesses to the event or historical period

research (REE-surch) to look for information on a topic

Find Out More

BOOKS

Fontichiaro, Kristin. *Go Straight to the Source.* Ann Arbor, MI: Cherry Lake, 2010.

Hamilton, John. *Primary and Secondary Sources.* Edina, MN: ABDO Publishing Company, 2005.

WEB SITES

Library of Congress—Using Primary Sources

www.loc.gov/teachers/usingprimarysources

Look here for important points to keep in mind when evaluating primary sources.

The U.S. National Archives and Records Administration—Photo Analysis Worksheet

www.archives.gov/education/lessons/worksheets/photo.html

Analyzing a primary source photograph? Use this helpful chart to organize your thoughts and observations.

Index

About the Author

Kristin Fontichiaro works at the University of Michigan School of Information. She used to be an elementary school librarian. She has written several books for teachers and librarians. This is her fourth book for children.